2ND EDITION

BERKLEE MUSIC THEORY

BOOK

1

BASIC PRINCIPLES OF RHYTHM, SCALES, AND INTERVALS

PAUL SCHMELING

Edited by Susan Gedutis Lindsay

CD INCLUDED

Audio Production Consultant: Mike Carrera
Voiceover Artist: Phil Ruokis

Berklee Media

Vice President: Dave Kusek
Dean of Continuing Education: Debbie Cavalier
Business Manager: Rob Green
Technology Manager: Mike Serio
Marketing Manager, Berkleemusic: Barry Kelly
Senior Graphic Designer: David Ehlers

Berklee Press

Senior Writer/Editor: Jonathan Feist
Senior Writer/Editor: Susan Gedutis Lindsay
Production Manager: Shawn Girsberger
Marketing Manager, Berklee Press: Jennifer D'Angora
Product Marketing Manager: David Goldberg
Production Assistant: Louis O'choa

ISBN 978-0-87639-110-5

1140 Boylston Street
Boston, MA 02215-3693 USA
(617) 747-2146

Visit Berklee Press Online at
www.berkleepress.com

DISTRIBUTED BY

HAL•LEONARD®
CORPORATION
7777 W. BLUEMOUND RD. P.O. BOX 13819
MILWAUKEE, WISCONSIN 53213

Visit Hal Leonard Online at
www.halleonard.com

Printed in the United States of America

Contents

10/10

CD Track List

Introduction

Berklee Music Theory, Book 1 teaches you how to read and understand music, using an approach I've developed through more than forty years of teaching at Berklee College of Music. Unlike most books on music theory, this book begins with the most basic aspect of contemporary music: rhythm. Reflecting the way we teach at Berklee, this book continues with a rigorous, hands-on, "ears-on" exploration of the inner workings of music, presenting notes, scales, and sounds as they are heard in jazz, blues, and popular music.

Whether you are a beginner or a more experienced musician who wants to learn more, you'll develop music listening, reading, and writing skills through exercises and ear training practice. I encourage you to work with a real keyboard, but if you don't have access to one, you can use the cut-out keyboard at the back of this book.

By the end of the book, you'll be able to read musical notes on a staff, write and use correct rhythm notation, and construct scales and intervals—and recognize them by ear. You will have the sounds and understanding you can use immediately to become a more effective musician.

—Paul Schmeling

Chair Emeritus, Piano Department

Berklee College of Music

Lesson 1. Pulse and Meter

A regular pulse **(beat)** is fundamental to music. It establishes the tempo—how fast or slow the music is played. The pulse is usually divided into groups of beats. Each group of beats is called a **measure** (bar). On the musical staff, **bar lines** separate measures. Longer compositions end with a final bar line.

The Musical Staff

The **staff** is where music notation is written. It includes five parallel lines and the four spaces between them. The lines and spaces of a staff are referred to by number, and are always counted from the bottom up. The percussion clef sign appears at the beginning of this staff; it is most commonly used for rhythmic notation.

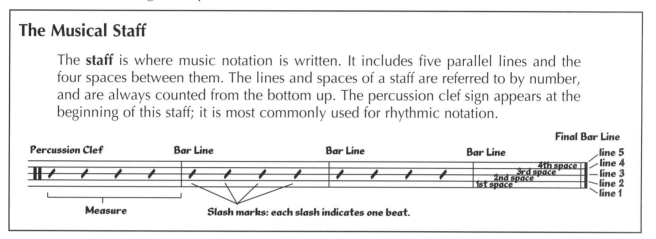

When beats are grouped into measures, the pulse is said to be in **meter**. Meter is indicated by a time signature. The **time signature** has two numbers, one above the other, and appears at the beginning of the first line of music.

The top number of the time signature indicates how many beats are in each measure, and the bottom number indicates the duration of each beat. (You'll learn more about duration in lesson 2.)

$\frac{4}{4}$ time is also known as "common time," because it is used so often. Common time is indicated with a **C**. **C** and $\frac{4}{4}$ mean the same thing: four beats per measure.

The first beat of a measure is called the **downbeat.** It is stressed more than the other beats. When words are set to music, usually the accented syllables are placed on the downbeats.

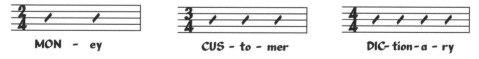

Sometimes, the accented syllable is not the first syllable of a word, as in the word "guiTAR," "comPUter," and "satisFACtion." In cases like these, the beat on which the word begins may be shifted to the previous measure. This allows the accented syllable to fall on the downbeat.

1

Practice

Circle the best rhythm for the following words, and underline the accented syllables.

Lesson 2. Notes

Notes are the building blocks of music. A note's length **(duration)** is measured in beats.

Whole notes last for four beats, which is a whole measure in $\frac{4}{4}$ meter. The symbol for a whole note is an open notehead.

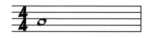

 2 On track 2, the piano plays whole notes and the metronome (click track) plays every beat. Listen carefully to hear both instruments.

Half notes last for half as long as whole notes: two beats in $\frac{4}{4}$ time. Their symbol is an open notehead with a vertical line called a stem.

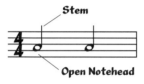

3 On track 3, the piano plays half notes and the metronome plays every beat.

Quarter notes last for a quarter of a whole note: one beat. Their symbol is a closed notehead with a stem.

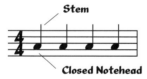

 4 On track 4, the piano and the metronome play quarter notes, that is, every beat together.

Practice

1. Practice writing one whole note in each measure. Notice the oval shape (not a circle) and its placement at the beginning of the measure.

2. Practice writing half notes in the measures provided.

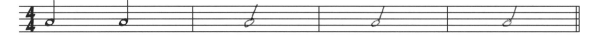

3. Practice writing quarter notes in the measures provided.

4. Circle the measure that has the correct number of beats.

5. Add bar lines to make three measures of $\frac{4}{4}$. All measures should be the same size.

6. Add bar lines to make four measures of $\frac{3}{4}$. All measures should be the same size.

7. Add bar lines to make six measures of $\frac{2}{4}$. All measures should be the same size.

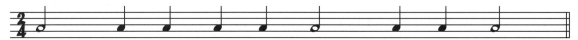

Lesson 3. Rests

Rests are used to indicate silence, just as notes are used to indicate sound. Like notes, rests can last for any number of beats.

Whole rests represent four beats of silence. Their symbol is a small, solid rectangle that hangs down from the fourth line up from the bottom of the staff.

5 On track 5, the piano plays whole notes and is silent for four beats during whole rests. The metronome plays every beat.

Half rests last for two beats. Their symbol is a small rectangle that lies on top of the third line up from the bottom of the staff.

6 On track 6, the piano plays half notes and is silent for two beats during half rests. The metronome plays every beat.

Quarter rests last for one beat. Their symbol looks like a sideways W with a thick middle.

7 On track 7, the piano plays quarter notes and is silent during quarter rests. The metronome plays every beat.

Practice

1. Practice writing whole rests in the measures provided. Unlike the whole note, the whole rest is placed in the middle of the measure.

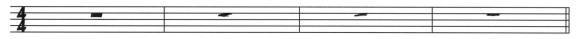

2. Practice writing half rests in the measures provided, two per measure. Notice that the rest value is placed on the line and each is equally spaced in its own half of the measure.

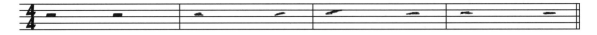

3. Practice writing quarter rests in the measures provided, four to a measure.

4. Circle the correct measure.

5. Add bar lines to make three measures of $\frac{4}{4}$.

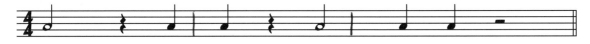

6. Add bar lines to make four measures of $\frac{3}{4}$.

7. Add bar lines to make six measures of $\frac{2}{4}$.

Exercises, Lessons 1–3. Rhythm, Notes, and Rests

1. Add whole, half, or quarter **note** values to complete the incomplete measures. Pay attention to spacing within the measure in choosing where to place the missing note values.

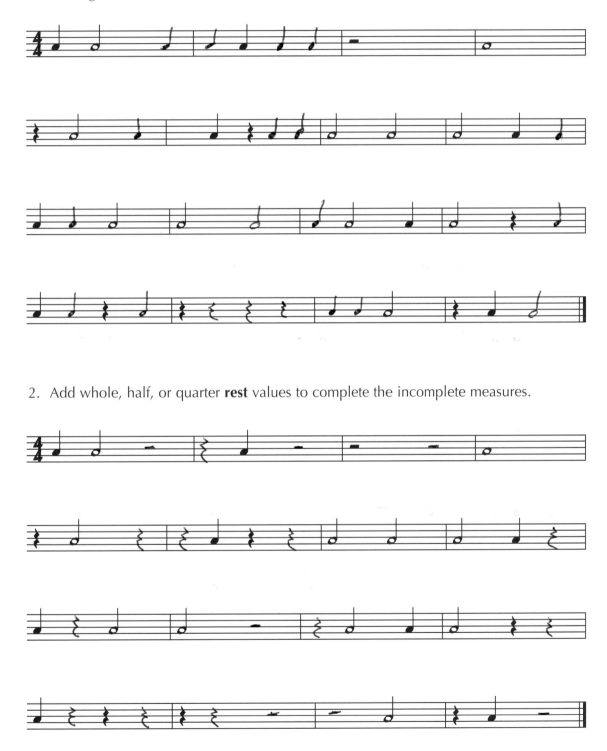

2. Add whole, half, or quarter **rest** values to complete the incomplete measures.

Ear Training

Important Note: Most of these ear training examples will begin with a two-measure countoff. In $\frac{4}{4}$ time, the countoff will be two slow clicks in the first measure, followed by four fast clicks in the second measure, as shown below. (Do not include the countoff measures in your answer.)

Measure:	**1**				**2**			
You hear:	click	(silence)	click	(silence)	click	click	click	click
Corresponds to count:	1	2	3	4	1	2	3	4

8 1. Listen to $\frac{4}{4}$ meter. How many measures of $\frac{4}{4}$ do you hear? Circle the correct answer.

    a. 4 ③ 2   b. 4 3 ②   c. ④ 3 2

9 2. Listen to whole notes for four measures, then half notes for two measures, then quarter notes for two measures. Then, listen to the examples and write (transcribe) these 2-measure rhythms. Each rhythm will be played twice, and there will be no break before the repeat.

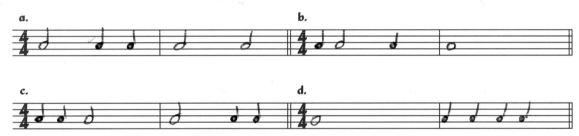

3. Listen to whole rests, half rests, and quarter rests. Rests will alternate with notes on the piano. Then, transcribe these 2-measure rhythms, which include both notes and rests. Each 2-measure exercise will be repeated. Remember to account for the countoff!

10

Lesson 4. Eighth Notes and Rests

The **eighth note** has the duration of half a quarter note. Eighth notes have a closed notehead, a stem, and a flag.

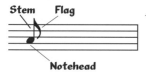

Eighth notes subdivide each quarter-note pulse into two equal parts—counted as "1 + 2 + 3 + 4 +" (say "and" for +). Eighth notes occur either "on the beat" or "off the beat." The off-beat is also referred to as the "and" of the beat.

11 On track 11, the piano plays eighth notes and the metronome plays every beat.

Eighth rests also last for half a quarter note or quarter rest. They look like this:

12 Play track 12 to hear eighth rests alternating with eighth notes. The piano plays the eighth note and the metronome plays every beat. Count aloud as you listen. Be sure to continue counting through the rest values.

Practice

1. Write eighth notes in the measures provided, eight per measure. Notice the length of the stem, the shape of the flag, and their equal placement within the measure.

2. Write eighth rests in the measures provided. Notice their shape and equal placement within the measure.

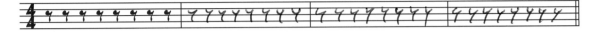

3. Circle the measure that has the correct number of note and rest values for the time signature.

4. Add bar lines to form four measures of $\frac{3}{4}$.

5. Add bar lines to form three measures of $\frac{4}{4}$.

6. Add bar lines to form six measures of $\frac{2}{4}$.

Lesson 5. Beaming Eighth Notes

Successive eighth notes are generally connected with a **beam,** instead of each note having individual flags. The beam is a thick horizontal line connecting the tops of the eighth note stems.

The beams do not cross over the third beat. In $\frac{4}{4}$, it is customary to start a new beam group at beat 3, as though an imaginary line divides the bar in half between beats 2 and 3.

Practice

1. Write beamed eighth notes in the measures provided.

2. Rewrite the beamed eighth notes on the blank staff so they do not cross over beat 3.

3. Rewrite the following rhythms using beamed eighths instead of separate flags. Be careful not to beam over the third beat, and keep the same note and rest values.

Lesson 6. Dots and Ties

Dots and ties increase a note's duration.

A **dot** increases a note's value by half of the note's duration. For example, a dotted half note lasts for three beats: two for the half note, plus half of that duration (a quarter note) for the dot.

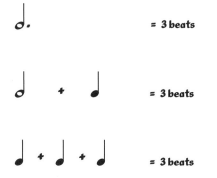

The dotted quarter note lasts for one and a half beats: one beat for the quarter note, plus half a beat (an eighth note) for the dot.

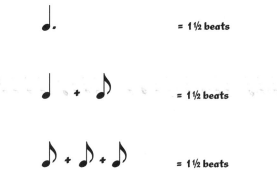

13 Play track 13 to hear an example of dotted rhythm values. Count carefully as you listen.

If the notehead is in a space, the dot is placed to the right in that same space; if on a line, the dot is placed in the space above.

A **tie** combines the durations of two or more notes. Ties and stems are always placed on opposite sides of the notehead. (Rests cannot be tied.)

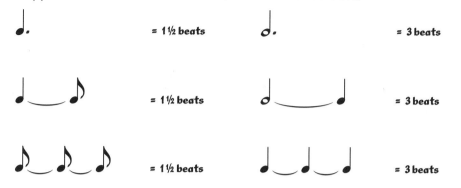

Practice

1. Practice writing dotted notes in the measures provided.

2. Add one note value to complete each measure.

3. Notate the following rhythm using dotted note values instead of ties. Do not change the duration or beat on which any note begins.

4. Practice tying notes that are on the same line or space.

Exercises, Lessons 4–6. Eighth Notes, Dots, and Ties

1. Add one note value to complete each measure.

2. Add one rest value to complete each measure.

3. Rewrite the rhythms on the blank staff, correcting beaming errors. Beam successive eighth notes where appropriate.

Ear Training

14   1.   Listen to whole, half, quarter, and eighth notes, then transcribe these 2-measure rhythms.

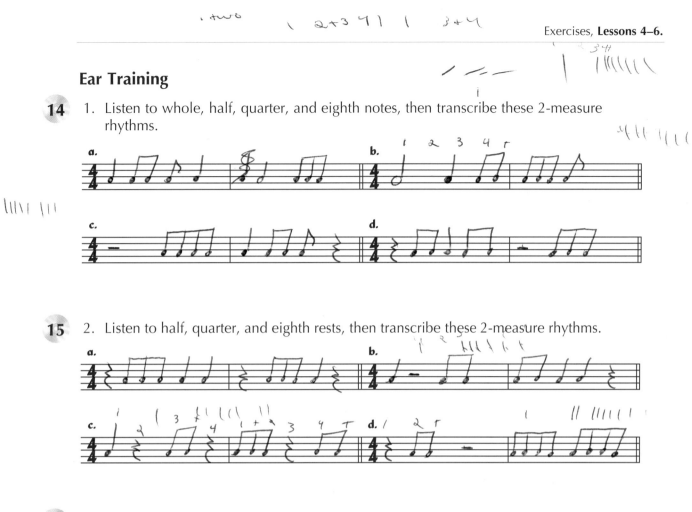

15   2.   Listen to half, quarter, and eighth rests, then transcribe these 2-measure rhythms.

16   3.   Listen to these dotted/tied note values, then transcribe these 2-measure rhythms.

Lesson 7. Rhythmic Notation Guidelines

The same rhythm can be written in different ways. Always try to use the simplest way so the notation is easy to read. Here are some basic guidelines.

Guideline 1: It is usually better to use one note or rest of longer duration than to tie together two or more smaller values.

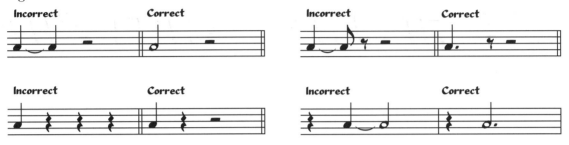

Guideline 2: Think of each $\frac{4}{4}$ measure as being divided into two halves, between beats 2 and 3. Complete each side of the measure, keeping the third beat visible.

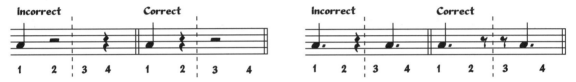

Guideline 3: Only half notes or larger can be written over the imaginary line between beats 2 and 3—and only if they begin on the beat.

This rule does not apply to rest values.

The examples below do not begin "on the beat" and are considered incorrect. The correct notation keeps the same durational values but is written so as to show the third beat.

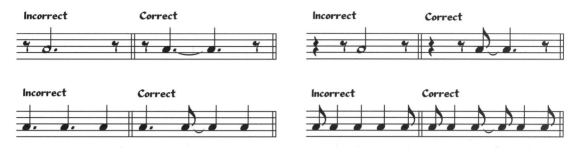

Practice

Rewrite these rhythms, correcting notation errors.

Lesson 8. Eighth-Note and Eighth-Rest Placement

When a beat is subdivided into an eighth note and a rest, the subdivided beat should be completed with an eighth note or rest before the next beat begins. Quarter rests and half rests should always begin *on the beat,* never on the "and" of a beat.

The incorrect example below shows a quarter rest that begins on the "and" of a beat. In the correct version, the first eighth rest completes beat 1 and the second eighth rest begins on beat 2.

In the next example, the incorrect measure shows a quarter rest that begins on the "and" of beat 3. To correct this, the quarter rest is shifted to represent beat 3, and the eighth rest and note together complete beat 4.

Practice

1. Complete each incomplete measure with rest values. Be careful to complete each subdivided beat before beginning the next one.

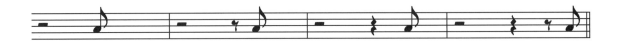

2. Rewrite the following rhythms on the blank staff, correcting notational errors.

Lesson 9. Other Time Signatures

As we have learned, the top number of a time signature indicates how many beats are in the measure.

The bottom number indicates the duration of each beat. If "4" is on the bottom, the beat is a quarter note long. If "2" is on the bottom, the beat is a half note long. If "8" is on the bottom, the beat is an eighth note long.

17 Sometimes, the meter and time signature change within a piece of music. When this happens, usually the note value that receives the beat (bottom number in the time signature) remains the same, but the number of beats per measure (top number) changes.

Practice

1. Add one rest value to complete each measure.

2. Add just one note value to complete each measure.

Exercises, Lessons 7–9. Notation and Time Signatures

Ear Training

18 1. Listen to $\frac{3}{4}$ meter for four measures. Then, transcribe these two 4-measure rhythms, which change from $\frac{3}{4}$ to $\frac{4}{4}$ time. There is a 2-measure countoff in $\frac{3}{4}$ meter in each measure.

19 2. Listen to $\frac{2}{4}$ meter for four measures. Then, transcribe these 4-measure rhythms, which change from $\frac{2}{4}$ to $\frac{3}{4}$ time. Note the 2-measure countoff in $\frac{2}{4}$ meter.

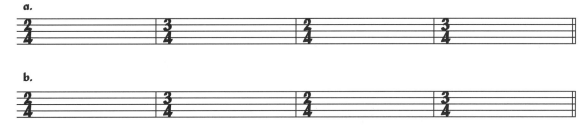

20 3. Listen to $\frac{5}{4}$ meter for four measures. Then, listen and write these 4-measure rhythms, which change from $\frac{4}{4}$ to $\frac{5}{4}$.

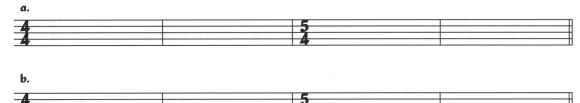

Lesson 10. Pitch Notation

Notes are placed on the lines and in the spaces of the staff according to their **pitch**. Pitch refers to how high or low a note sounds.

Notes higher on the staff sound higher in pitch. Notes lower on the staff sound lower in pitch, as shown below. The highest and lowest notes on the staff below are labeled. Listen to these low notes and high notes on track 21.

Ledger Lines

If the pitch is very high or very low, the staff can be extended using **ledger lines**. These are used for notes outside of the staff's range.

Practice

Mark the highest and lowest note on the staff with "H" and "L."

Lesson 11. The Treble Clef

A **clef sign** is placed at the beginning of the staff to indicate the pitch of a specific staff line or space. The most commonly used clefs are the G clef and the F clef.

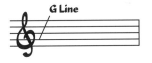 = G clef

The **G clef,** also called **treble clef,** indicates that the second line on the staff is G. Note that the bottom loop surrounds the G line on the staff.

Reading Treble Clef

Notes are named with the letters A, B, C, D, E, F, and G. Once G is reached, start over with A again.

In treble clef, the notes from G upward are G, A, B, C, D, E, F, and G. The notes from G downward are G, F, E, and D.

The range may be extended using ledger lines:

Stem Direction

The direction of stems on noteheads written in treble clef depends on where the notes are located on the staff. Notes placed on or above the middle line (B) are notated with stems down. Notes placed on or below the middle line are notated with stems up. Notice that the stems are attached to the right side of the notehead if up and the left side if down.

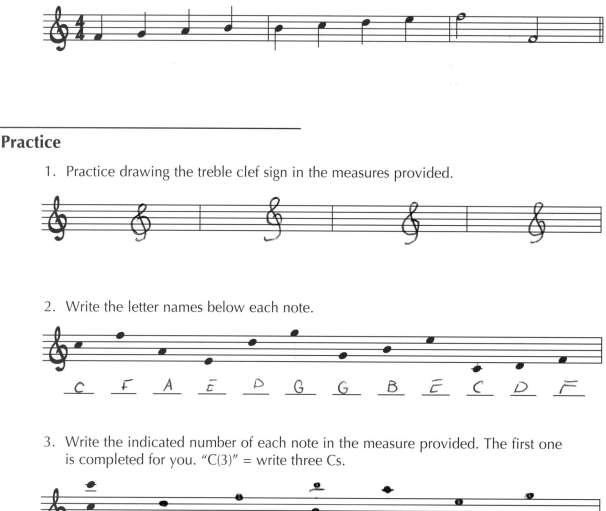

Practice

1. Practice drawing the treble clef sign in the measures provided.

2. Write the letter names below each note.

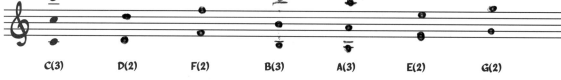

   C   F   A   E   D   G   G   B   E   C   D   F

3. Write the indicated number of each note in the measure provided. The first one is completed for you. "C(3)" = write three Cs.

   C(3)   D(2)   F(2)   B(3)   A(3)   E(2)   G(2)

4. Add stems to the following noteheads.

Lesson 12. The Bass Clef

The **F clef** indicates the F line on a staff by placing its two dots on either side of the fourth line. It is also called **bass clef** (pronounced "base").

𝄢 = bass clef

Bass Clef Notes

In bass clef, the notes from F upward are F, G, A, and B. Downward from F, they are F, E, D, C, B, A, G, and F.

The range may be extended using ledger lines:

Stem direction for the bass clef is determined the same way as in treble: notes placed on or above the middle line (D) are notated with stems down; notes placed on or below the middle line are notated with stems up.

Practice

1. Practice drawing the bass clef sign in the measures provided.

2. Identify the letter names of these bass clef notes.

A   F   A   G   G   A   D   C   B   F   G   C

3. Write the number of notes indicated on the staff provided.

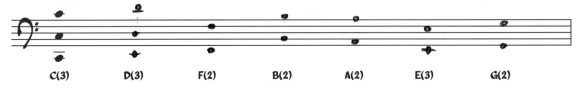

C(3)   D(3)   F(2)   B(2)   A(2)   E(3)   G(2)

4. Add stems to the following noteheads.

Lesson 13. The Grand Staff

The treble and bass clefs are frequently used together in what is known as the **grand staff.** Notice on the grand staff that middle C is on the ledger line between the two staffs. The grand staff is used for piano music and for studies of theory.

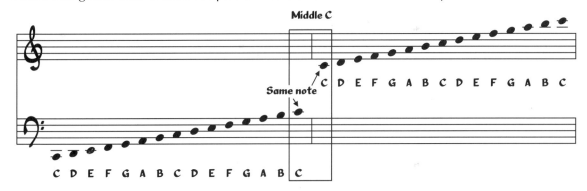

Octaves

We have seen that there are seven letter names for the notes: A, B, C, D, E, F, and G. After the seventh note, the letters repeat, only in a higher **octave.** The following shows the note G in four different octaves.

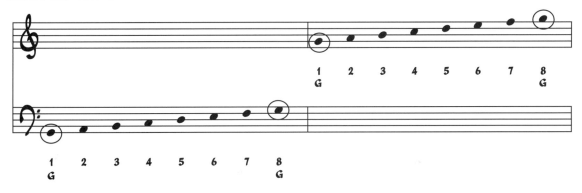

22 Listen to the sound of a note and its octaves.

Practice

1. Write a note that is one octave lower than the note given. Use the bass clef provided.

2. Write a note that is one octave higher than the note given. Use the treble clef provided.

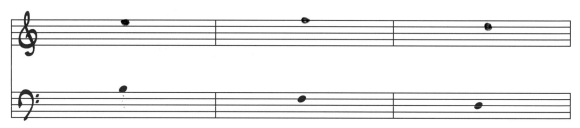

3. Write a note that is two octaves lower than the note given. Use the bass clef provided.

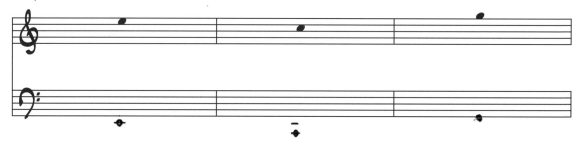

4. Write a note that is two octaves higher than the note given. Use the treble clef provided.

Lesson 14. Accidentals

Accidentals are symbols that alter a note's pitch.

Sharps

23 The sharp sign (♯) raises a note's pitch by a half step, the next higher note on the keyboard. This note may be a white or a black key. (H = half step)

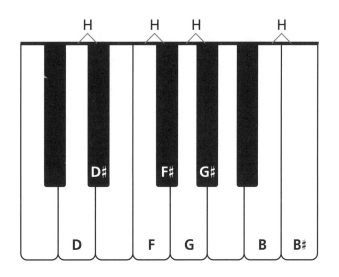

Flats

24 The flat sign (♭) lowers a note's pitch by a half step, the next lower note on the keyboard. This note could be a white or a black key.

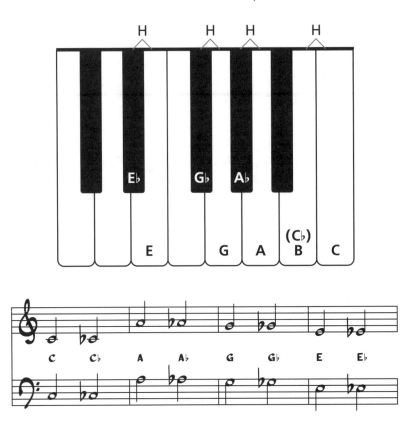

Naturals

The natural sign (♮) indicates that a note is neither sharp nor flat. On a staff, the appearance of a natural sign cancels out a sharp or flat that has been previously applied to a note.

Rules for Accidentals

Once introduced into a measure, accidentals are in effect for the entire measure but are cancelled out by the bar line. In the following example, every E in the first measure is flat because of the introduced flat sign. The E in the second measure is an E natural, with no natural sign needed.

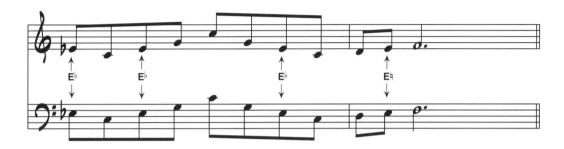

Practice

1. Use the appropriate note and accidental to raise each note by a half step. The first one is done for you.

2. Use the appropriate note and accidental to lower each note by a half step.

Lesson 15. Key Signatures

Key signatures, placed at the beginning of a piece of music, are a way to indicate that certain accidentals will be in use throughout the piece, which avoids the need for a written accidental each time the note appears. The key signature of three flats means that all B, A, and E notes will be flat. If we want an E natural, a natural sign is needed, as in measure 2 below.

Sharp signs in key signatures are written in this order, from left to right: F♯, C♯, G♯, D♯, A♯, E♯, and B♯. Notice the placement of these sharp signs.

Flat signs in key signatures are written in this order, from left to right: B♭, E♭, A♭, D♭, G♭, C♭, and F♭. Notice the placement of these flat signs.

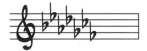

Practice

1. Practice writing the key signature of six sharps in the measures provided.

2. Practice writing the key signature of six flats in the measures provided.

Lesson 16. Enharmonic Equivalents

When notes are spelled differently (by a different letter), but have the same pitch and are the same key on the keyboard, they are known as **enharmonic equivalents,** or just **enharmonics.**

For example, a half step up from F is F♯, and a half step down from G is G♭. Note that F♯ and G♭ are the same physical key on the keyboard. They are enharmonic equivalents. Also note that E and F, and B and C are a half step apart; there are no half steps between them.

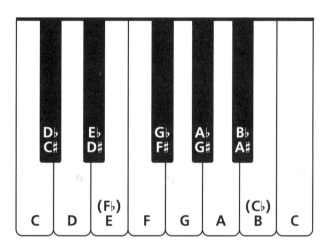

Here are some enharmonic equivalents:

Practice

1. Circle the measures that contain enharmonic equivalents.

2. Write the enharmonic equivalents to the notes given, in both treble and bass clef.

Exercises, Lessons 10–16. The Staff, Accidentals, and Key Signatures

1. Write this melody one octave lower in the bass clef provided.

2. Write this melody one octave higher in the treble clef provided.

3. Write the complete name (letter and accidental) of each note of this melody on the line between the staves.

G A♭ B♭ E♭ F A♭ D E♭ F B♭ C D E♭

key of E →

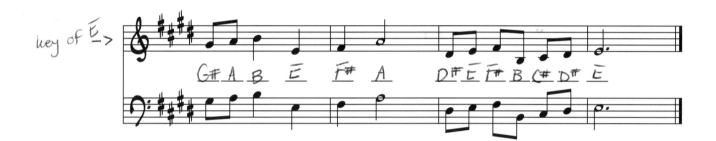

G♯ A B E F♯ A D♯ E F♯ B C♯ D♯ E

key of G →

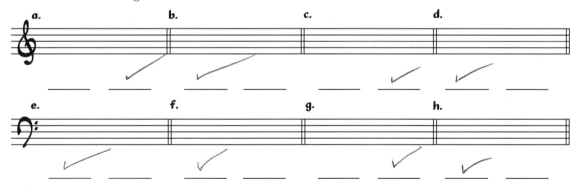

G A B E F♯ A D♯ E F♯ B C♯ D♯ E

Ear Training

25 1. Which note is higher?

a.   b.   c.   d.

e.   f.   g.   h.

26   2. In each example, you will hear two notes. If the second note is a half step higher or half step lower, write the second note with the appropriate accidental in the space provided. If the notes are the same pitch, then write the second note, spelled with its enharmonic name.

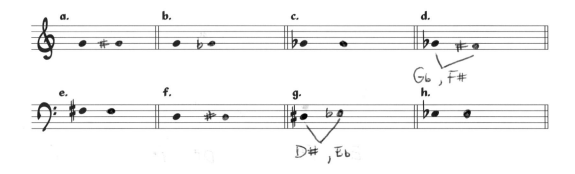

Lesson 17. Half Steps and Whole Steps

 27 The **whole step** is the distance of two half steps. On the keyboard, two keys a whole step apart have one key between them.

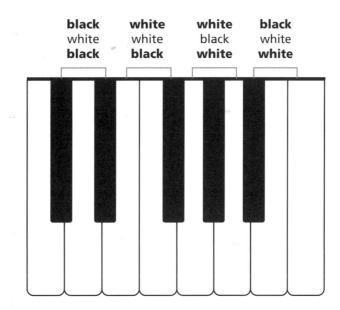

 27 On the keyboard, keys next to each other, with no other key in between, whether white or black, are a **half step** apart, as you saw in lesson 14.

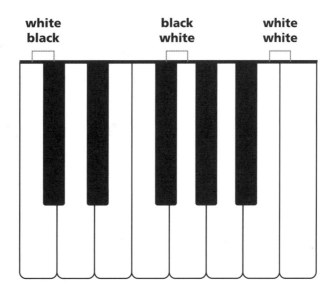

Practice

In each of these examples, the first one is done for you.

1. Write a note on the staff that is a half step above each given note. As practice, use the adjacent letter name. For example, to identify the note a half step up from F, instead of writing F♯, use the adjacent letter name, G♭.

2. Write a note that is a half step below each given note. Again, use the adjacent letter name.

3. Write a note that is a whole step above each given note.

4. Write a note that is a whole step below each given note.

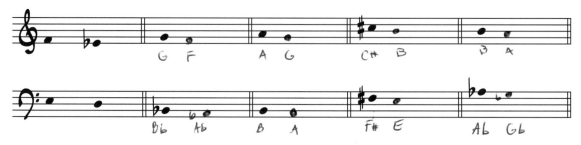

Lesson 18. The Chromatic Scale

A series of notes that move in a consistent direction, and begin and end on the same note, is called a **scale.** There are many kinds of scales.

The **chromatic scale** moves by half steps up or down and can begin on any note. It has twelve notes. Listen to the chromatic scale on track 28.

 The ascending chromatic scale uses sharps to help point in the upward direction of the scale.

The descending chromatic scale uses flats to point in the downward direction of the scale.

Practice

1. Write an ascending chromatic scale starting on the note given. Remember to raise (sharp) notes in order to point the scale upwards.

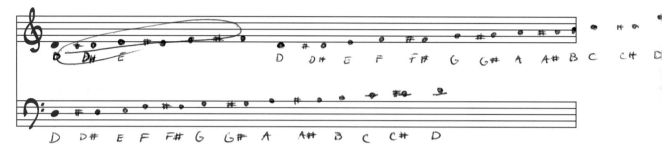

2. Write a descending chromatic scale starting on the note given. Remember to lower (flat) notes in order to point the downward direction.

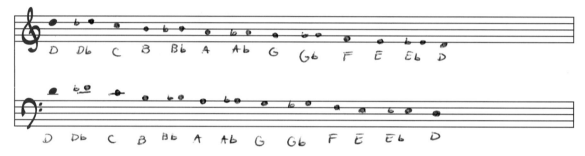

Lesson 19. The Whole-Tone Scale

The **whole-tone scale** moves by whole steps up or down and can begin on any note. There are only six different notes in a whole-tone scale, so one of the letter names does not appear in the scale. Note there is no B in the example below.

29 The ascending whole-tone scale looks like this. It can start on any note. This one starts on C, and uses sharp signs to point in the upward direction.

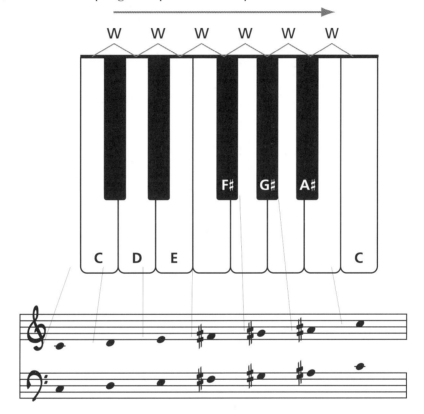

The descending whole-tone scale looks like this. It uses flat signs to point in the downward direction.

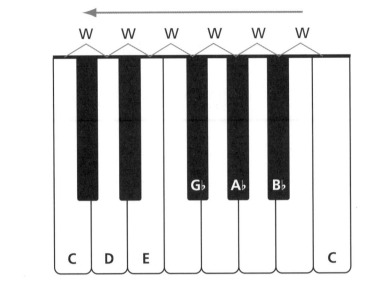

Practice

1. Write an ascending whole-tone scale starting with the note given.

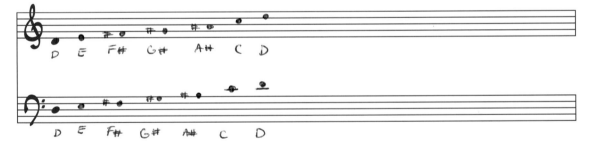

2. Write a descending whole-tone scale starting with the note given.

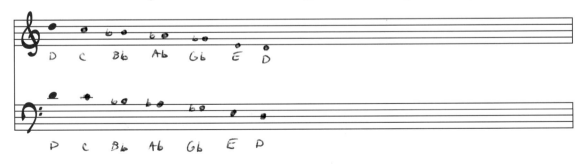

Exercises, Lessons 17–19. Half Steps and Whole Steps

1. Identify the notes in each measure as either a half step (H) or whole step (W) apart.

W   H   H   W   H   W   W   H

w   H   H   W   H   W   W   H

Ear Training

30

1. Listen to whole steps and half steps, then circle the correct answer, half step or whole step.

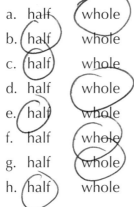

a. half   **whole**
b. **half**   whole
c. **half**   whole
d. half   **whole**
e. **half**   whole
f. half   **whole**
g. half   **whole**
h. **half**   whole

31

2. Listen to chromatic and whole-tone scales. Identify each example as part of either a whole-tone scale or chromatic scale by circling the correct answer.

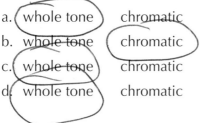

a. **whole tone**   chromatic
b. whole tone   **chromatic**
c. **whole tone**   chromatic
d. **whole tone**   chromatic

Lesson 20. The Major Scale

The most common scale in Western music is the **major scale.** Here is the C major scale. The major scale uses all seven letter names successively, with none repeating until the octave. Listen to its sound.

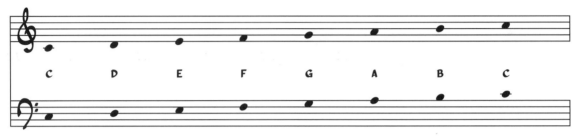

32 Listen to the major scale on track 32.

The notes follow this pattern of whole steps (W) and half steps (H):

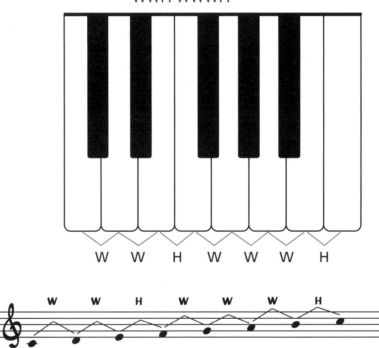

Practice

1. Write out the F major scale using the whole-step/half-step formula. You will need one accidental. Remember: use all seven letter names.

F   G   A   A#   C   D   E   F
W   W   H   W   W   W   H

F   G   A   A#   C   D   E   F

2. Write out the G major scale. Again, you will need one accidental.

G   A   B   Cb   D   E   F#   G
W   W   H   W   W   W   H

G   A   B   C   D   E   F#   G

Lesson 21. Scale Degrees

The notes of the major scale can be identified by number, according to their place in the scale. Their location in the scale is called their **scale degree.** For example, D is the second note of the C major scale, and is called the "second scale degree," "scale degree 2," or just "2." Numbering starts with the bottom note (1) to the top note (7). Then, the bottom note—the **tonic**—is repeated an octave higher.

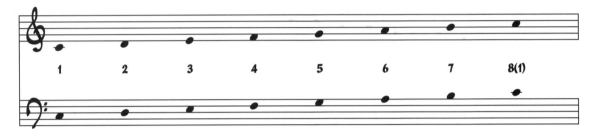

Syllable names are frequently used instead of numbers, especially for singing, because they are easier to sing than numbers.

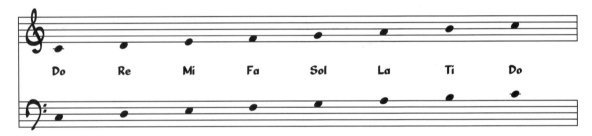

Practice

1. In each measure, write the note implied by the indicated scale and scale degree in both clefs. The first note is done for you.

2. In each measure, write the notes implied by the indicated scale and scale degree, in both clefs.

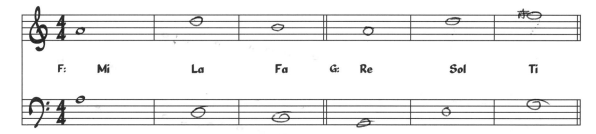

Lesson 22. Major Scales Using Sharps

Following the pattern of whole steps and half steps for a major scale, you discovered that the G major scale uses one sharp. You'll discover the other major scales that use sharps by completing the practice exercises below.

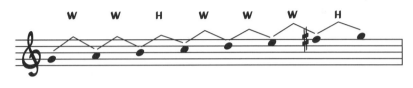

Practice

1. Complete each major scale, beginning on the given tonics and using the WWH WWWH pattern discussed. The number of sharps needed for each is indicated. Remember to use all letter names successively.

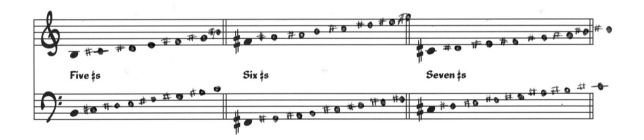

2. Write the key signature for the following major scales.

Lesson 23. Major Scales Using Flats

As you learned in lesson 20, the F major scale uses one flat.

You'll explore the rest of the major scales that use flats in the exercises below.

Practice

1. Write a major scale beginning on each of the given tonics, using the pattern discussed. The number of flats needed for each key is indicated.

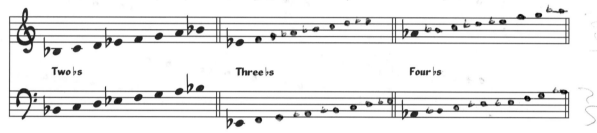

Two ♭s   Three ♭s   Four ♭s

Five ♭s   Six ♭s   Seven ♭s

2. Write the key signatures for the following major scales.

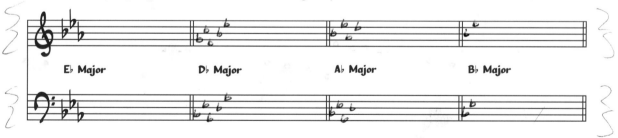

E♭ Major   D♭ Major   A♭ Major   B♭ Major

Exercises, Lessons 20–23. Major Scales

1. Using the note and scale degree information given, complete each major scale in both clefs, by writing both before and after the given note, as required. The first one is done for you.

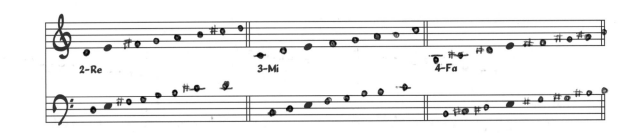

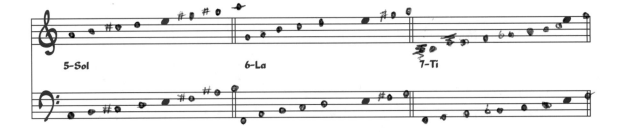

Ear Training

Listen to the first four notes of the major scale.

33

33 1. In examples (a)-(d) below, you will hear a series of four notes, repeated. The second repetition will have at least one note that is different from the original. Identify the note or notes that are different by marking accidentals in front of the appropriate notes in each second measure.

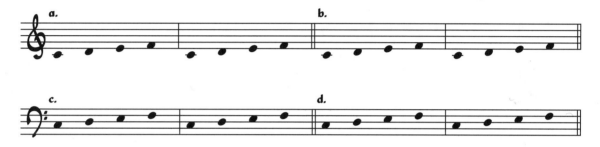

34 2. In examples (a) and (b) below, listen to the entire major scale repeated three times. In repetitions (i) and (ii), identify the notes that are different from the original, using the appropriate accidentals.

Lesson 24. The Natural Minor Scale

In the **natural minor scale,** scale degrees 3, 6, and 7 are a half step lower than the same scale degrees in the major scale. A natural minor scale based on the same note as the major is called its **parallel minor.** Listen and compare major to natural minor.

35 C minor is the parallel minor scale to C major:

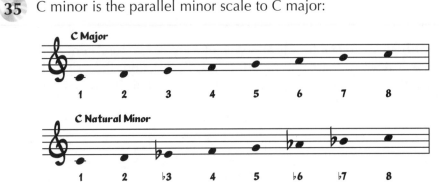

Practice

Write first the indicated major scale and then the parallel natural minor scale.

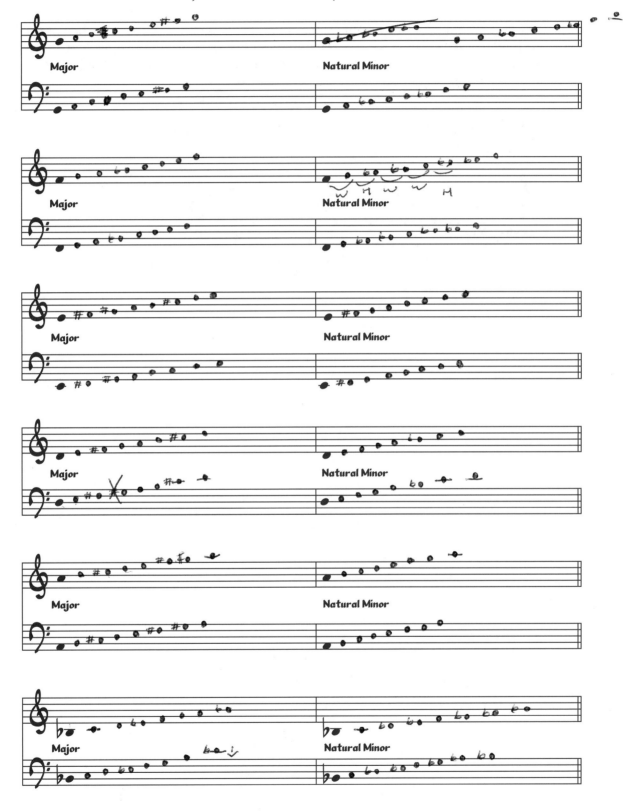

Lesson 25. The Relative Major/Minor Relationship

The natural minor scale uses the same notes as a major scale, except it begins and ends on La, scale degree 6. A natural minor scale, if built on scale degree 6 of a given major scale, is called that major scale's **relative minor.** The pattern of whole and half steps for natural minor is:

WH WWH WW

36 The scale A natural minor is the relative minor scale to C major:

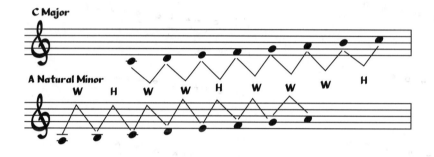

Practice

Write each indicated major scale and then its relative minor scale. The note in the second measure of each grouping below indicates the tonic note of the relative minor.

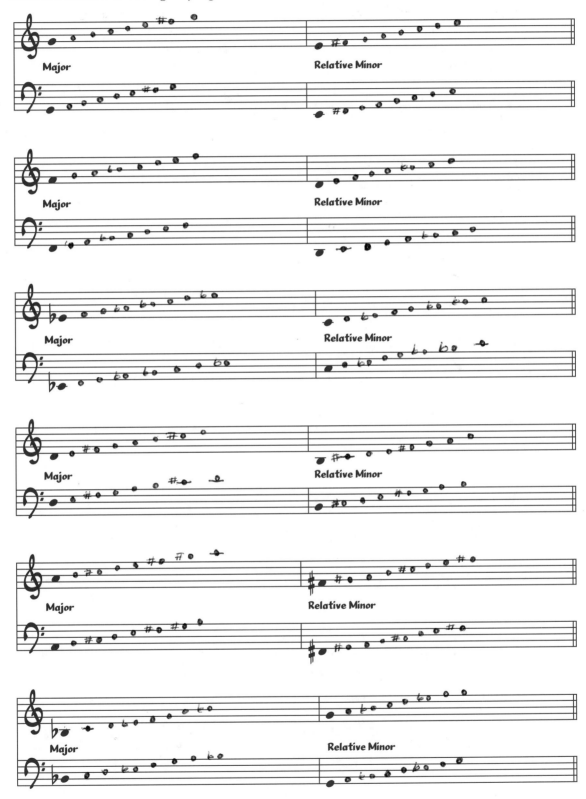

Lesson 26. Minor Scale Syllable Names

In comparing the major scale to the natural minor scale, the notes that are different use different syllable names. Mi becomes Me (pronounced "may"); La becomes Le (pronounced "lay"); and Ti becomes Te (pronounced "tay").

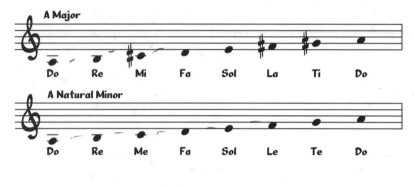

Practice

Write the note indicated by the given scale and syllable.

Exercises, Lessons 24–26. Minor Scales

1. Using the scale degree information given, complete each natural minor scale by writing both before and after the given note, as required.

Ear Training

37   1. Listen to the first five notes of the major scale and the first five notes of the minor scale. Then, identify each scale as either major or minor by circling the correct answer.

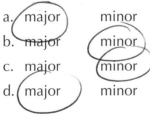

a. (major)   minor

b. ~~major~~   (minor)

c. major   (minor)

d. (major)   minor

38   2. Listen to the upper four notes of major and of natural minor, and identify each example as either major or natural minor.

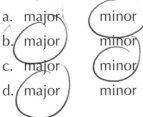

a. major   (minor)

b. (major)   minor

c. major   (minor)

d. (major)   minor

Lesson 27. The Harmonic Minor Scale

The **harmonic minor** scale is like natural minor, except that scale degree 7 is a half step higher.

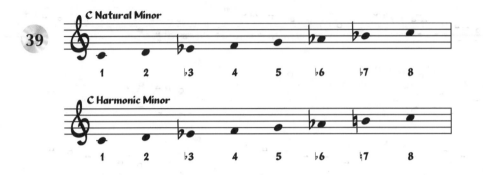

Practice

Write the natural minor scale, then the harmonic minor form.

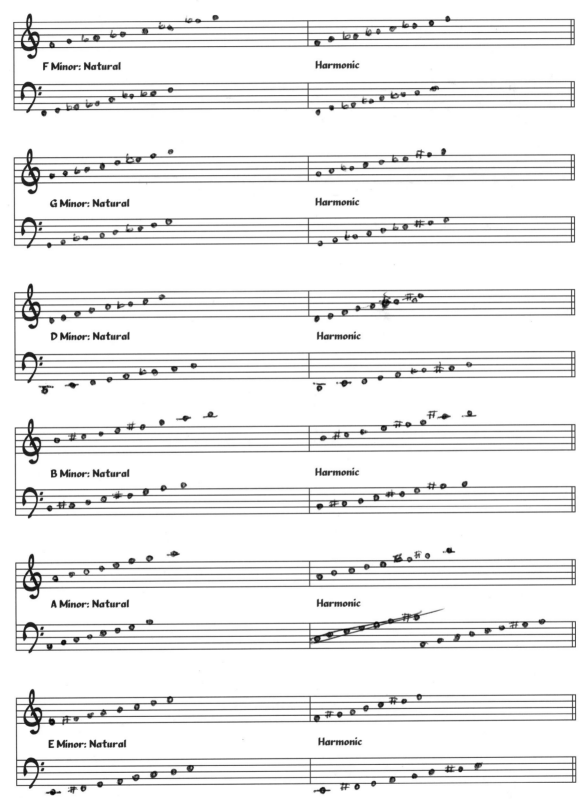

F Minor: Natural   Harmonic

G Minor: Natural   Harmonic

D Minor: Natural   Harmonic

B Minor: Natural   Harmonic

A Minor: Natural   Harmonic

E Minor: Natural   Harmonic

Lesson 28. The Ascending Melodic Minor Scale

The **ascending melodic minor** scale is like natural minor, except that scale degrees 6 and 7 are a half step higher. It looks like a major scale with a lowered 3.

Practice

Write the natural minor scale, then the ascending melodic minor form.

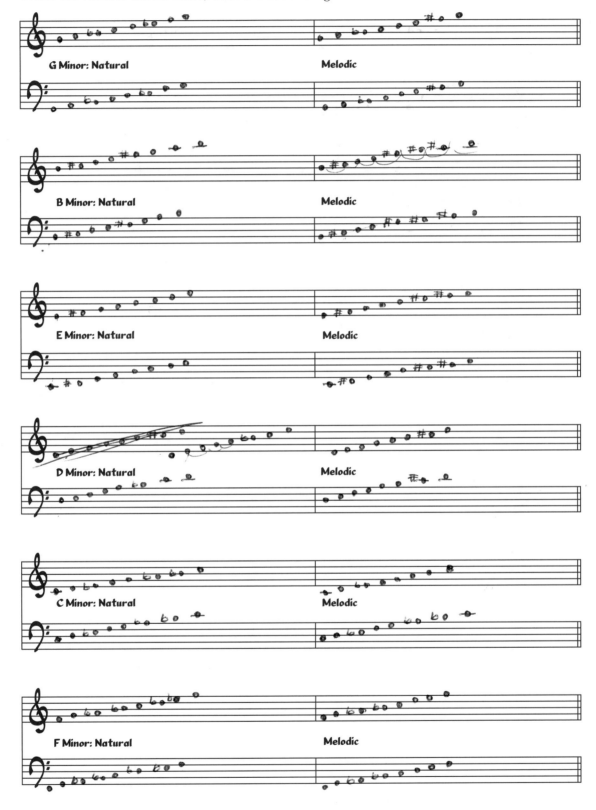

G Minor: Natural   Melodic

B Minor: Natural   Melodic

E Minor: Natural   Melodic

D Minor: Natural   Melodic

C Minor: Natural   Melodic

F Minor: Natural   Melodic

Lesson 29. The Descending Melodic Minor Scale

Melodic minor scales descend in two different ways. The **traditional melodic minor** scale descends with scale degrees 6 and 7 lowered by a half step, reverting back to the natural minor form.

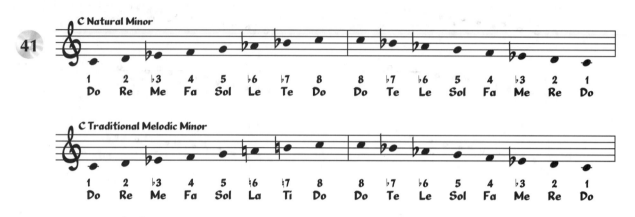

The **real melodic minor** descends just as it ascends, with scale degrees 6 and 7 raised.

Practice

Write the ascending melodic minor, then the descending traditional and real melodic minor forms.

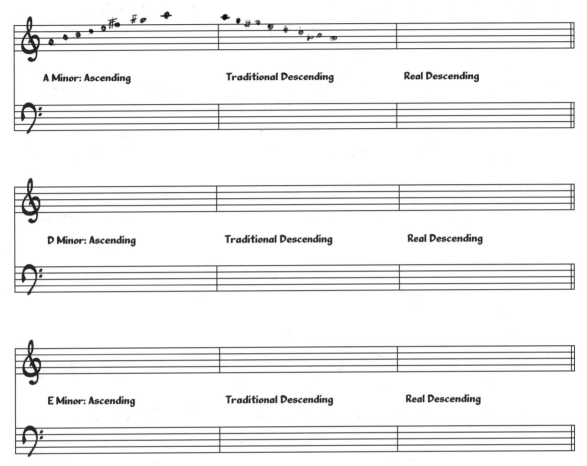

A Minor: Ascending   **Traditional Descending**   **Real Descending**

D Minor: Ascending   **Traditional Descending**   **Real Descending**

E Minor: Ascending   **Traditional Descending**   **Real Descending**

Lesson 30. Minor Scale Key Signatures

Minor keys use the key signature of their relative major, and introduce accidentals as needed for the harmonic and melodic minor forms.

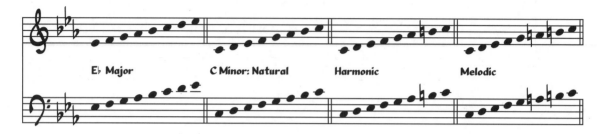

Practice

Write the key signature for each of these minor keys. Hint: First identify the relative major for each of these minor scales.

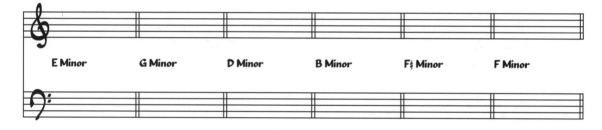

Exercises, Lessons 27–30. Harmonic and Melodic Minor Scales

1. Write the indicated minor scales, identifying the keys from the key signatures and using accidentals when required.

Harmonic   { Natural }   Ascending Melodic

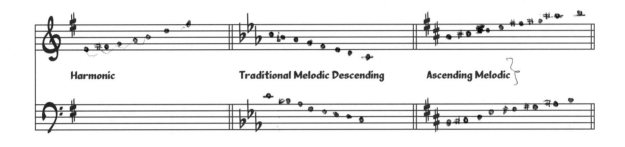

Harmonic   Traditional Melodic Descending   Ascending Melodic

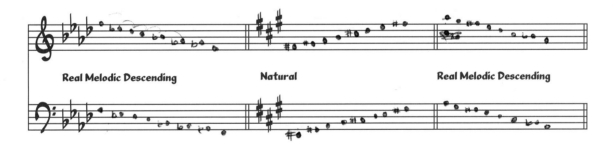

Real Melodic Descending   Natural   Real Melodic Descending

Ear Training

43   1. Listen to the natural minor scale. Compare the upper four notes of natural minor and harmonic minor. Then, identify each example as either natural or harmonic minor.

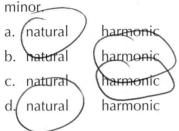

     a. (natural)   harmonic

     b. natural   (harmonic)

     c. natural   (harmonic)

     d. (natural)   harmonic

44   2. Listen to and compare the upper four notes of traditional melodic and real melodic minor. Then, identify each example as either traditional melodic or real melodic minor.

     a. traditional melodic   (real melodic)

     b. (traditional melodic)   real melodic

     c. traditional melodic   (real melodic)

     d. (traditional melodic)   real melodic

45   3. Identify each example as natural, harmonic, traditional melodic, or real melodic minor.

     a. natural   (harmonic)   traditional melodic   real melodic

     b. (natural)   harmonic   traditional melodic   real melodic

     c. natural   harmonic   (traditional melodic)   real melodic

     d. natural   (harmonic)   traditional melodic   real melodic

     e. (natural)   harmonic   (traditional melodic)   real melodic

     f. natural   harmonic   (traditional melodic)   real melodic

     g. natural   (harmonic)   traditional melodic   real melodic

     h. natural   harmonic   traditional melodic   (real melodic)

Lesson 31. Interval Naming

An **interval** is the distance between two notes. Like scale degrees, intervals are identified with numbers. These numbers are determined by counting letter names from one note to the next. For example, the interval from C up to G is a "fifth." C is counted as 1, then D is 2, E is 3, F is 4, and G makes 5, a fifth.

The interval from C down to G would be different. Starting with C as 1, count steps: B is 2, A is 3, and G makes 4. The interval from C down to G is a fourth.

An interval's notes can sound simultaneously (**harmonic**) or one note after the other (**melodic**).

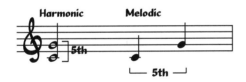

47 Listen to harmonic and melodic intervals on track 47.

Practice

1. Indicate the number name of each interval.

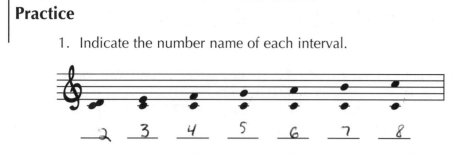

2. Complete each measure by writing a second half note that forms the indicated melodic interval above each note.

  5th   **3rd**   **4th**   **2nd**   **7th**

3. Complete each measure by writing a second half note that forms the indicated melodic interval below each note.

  7th   **6th**   **4th**   **3rd**   **2nd**

Lesson 32. Perfect and Major Intervals

Intervals often need a more detailed name than just the number. Unisons, fourths, fifths, and octaves are traditionally called **perfect intervals** when the upper note of the interval is within the major scale built on the lower note. "P" is the symbol used to indicate a perfect interval.

48

Perfect Unison   Perfect 4th (P4)   Perfect 5th (P5)   Perfect Octave

Seconds, thirds, sixths, and sevenths are traditionally called **major** when the upper note is within the major scale built on the lower note.

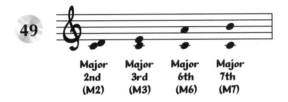

49

Major 2nd (M2)   Major 3rd (M3)   Major 6th (M6)   Major 7th (M7)

Practice

1. Write notes to form the four perfect intervals above each given note.

Perfect Unison   P4   P5   Perfect Octave   Perfect Unison   P4   P5   Perfect Octave

2. Write notes to form the four perfect intervals below each given note.

Perfect Unison   P4   P5   Perfect Octave   Perfect Unison   P4   P5   Perfect Octave

69

3. Write notes to form the four major intervals above each given note.

         M2   **M3**   **M6**   **M7**   **M2**   **M3**   **M6**   **M7**

4. Write notes to form the four major intervals below each given note.

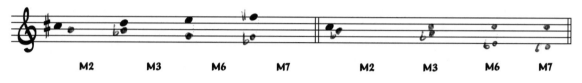

         M2   **M3**   **M6**   **M7**   **M2**   **M3**   **M6**   **M7**

Lesson 33. Major vs. Minor

Intervals a half step smaller than major are called **minor**. Lowering the upper note by a half step will form a minor interval from a major one.

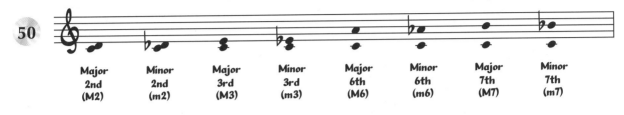

Raising the lower note by a half step will also form a minor interval from a major one.

Practice

1. Write the indicated major interval then the minor interval above each given note.

2. Write the indicated major interval then the minor interval below each given note.

3. Identify each interval with its complete name.

Minor 3rd   Major 6th   Minor 7th   Major 3rd   major 2nd minor 2nd

Lesson 34. Perfect and Diminished Intervals

Intervals a half step smaller than perfect intervals are called **diminished**. Lowering the upper note by a half step will form a diminished interval from a perfect one. The symbol for diminished is a °.

Raising the lower note by a half step also will form a diminished interval from a perfect one.

Practice

1. Write the indicated perfect interval then the diminished interval above each given note.

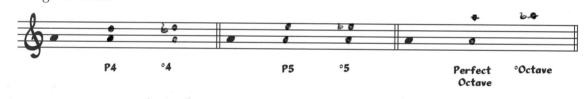

2. Write the indicated perfect interval then the diminished interval below each given note.

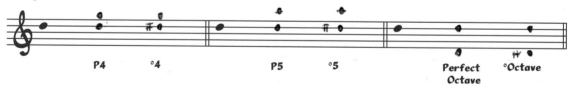

3. Identify each interval with its complete name.

Diminished 4th   P5   °Octave   P4   °5   °5

Lesson 35. Augmented Intervals

Both major and perfect intervals, when made a half step larger, are called **augmented,** abbreviated +.

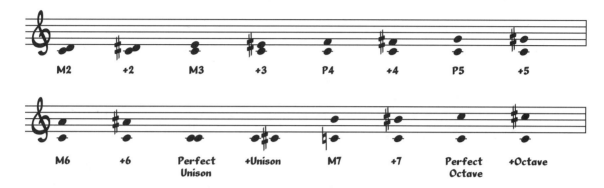

M2   +2   M3   +3   P4   +4   P5   +5

M6   +6   Perfect   +Unison   M7   +7   Perfect   +Octave
              Unison   Octave

Practice

1. Write the indicated intervals above each given note.

P4   +4   M3   +3   P5   +5   M7   +7

2. Write the indicated intervals below each given note.

M6   +6   M2   +2   P5   +5   Perfect   +Octave
                                    Octave

3. Identify each interval with its complete name.

Augmented 4th   ~~Augmented~~ 7th   major 6th   Augmented 5th
                  major

Augmented 2nd   Augmented 4th   Augmented 6th   Major Third

Lesson 36. Compound Intervals

Intervals whose notes are more than one octave apart are known as **compound intervals**. The compound second (an octave plus a second) becomes a ninth, a compound third becomes a tenth, a compound fourth becomes an eleventh, and so on. The terms perfect, major, and minor still apply, as though the notes were in the same octave.

Practice

1. Write the indicated interval above each given note.

2. Write the indicated interval below each given note.

3. Identify each interval with its complete compound name.

Exercises, Lessons 31–36. Intervals

1. Beginning with the C, write a note a major third lower, then a minor third lower than *that* note, until you have used all of the indicated intervals. If done correctly, the last note will be B♭. Then, do the same thing starting on A in the bass clef. If done correctly, the last note will be A.

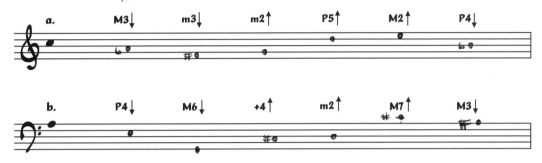

2. Use the grand staff to accommodate the notes of these compound intervals, moving in succession from the last note, as you did in the previous exercise.

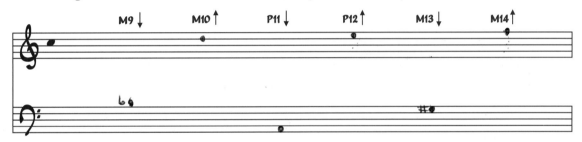

Ear Training

51 1. Listen to the major scale, then identify these intervals by name (m2, P5, M3, etc.).

a. _P5_   b. _m3_   c. _M6_   d. _P4_   e. _m2_   f. _M7_

52 2. Listen to major and minor seconds up and down. Then, identify each example as either a major second or minor second by circling the correct answer.

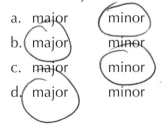

a. major minor

b. major minor

c. major minor

d. major minor

53 3. Listen to major and minor thirds up and down. Then, identify each example as either major or minor by circling the correct answer.

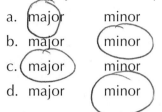

a. major   minor
b. major   minor
c. major   minor
d. major   minor

54 4. Listen to perfect and augmented fourths up and down. Then, identify each example as either a perfect or augmented fourth.

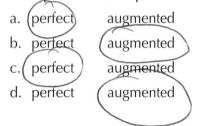

a. perfect   augmented
b. perfect   augmented
c. perfect   augmented
d. perfect   augmented

55 5. Listen to perfect and diminished fifths up and down. Then, identify each example as either a perfect or diminished fifth.

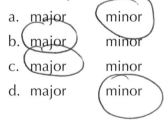

a. perfect   diminished
b. perfect   diminished
c. perfect   diminished
d. perfect   diminished

56 6. Listen to major and minor sixths up and down. Then, identify each example as either major or minor.

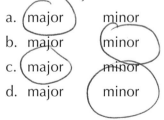

a. major   minor
b. major   minor
c. major   minor
d. major   minor

57 7. Listen to major and minor sevenths up and down. Then, identify each example as either major or minor.

a. major   minor
b. major   minor
c. major   minor
d. major   minor

What's Next?

Congratulations on finishing *Berklee Music Theory, Book 1*. Now that you have learned your notes, scales, and intervals, you're ready to progress to Book 2. In it, you'll learn about chords and chord types, including major, minor, diminished, and augmented triads and seventh chords. Then, you'll practice voice-leading, learning how to connect notes from chord to chord in a way that sounds smooth and musical. After an exploration of harmonic accompaniment on piano, you'll finish up by writing melodies of your own.

Until then—keep practicing, and continue to build your knowledge of music theory. It will make you a better musician today.

Answer Key

Page 2. Practice

   1. a

   2. b

   3. c

Page 4. Practice

   1–3. Writing exercises

   4.

   5.

   6.

   7.

Page 5. Practice

   1. Writing exercise

Page 6. Practice

   2–3. Writing exercises

   4.

   5.

6.

7.

Page 7. Exercises, Lessons 1–3

1.

2.

Page 8. Ear Training

1. (a) 3, (b) 2, (c) 4

2.

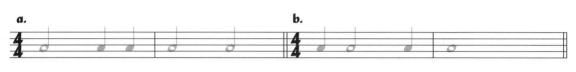

3.

Page 9. Practice

1. Writing exercise

Page 10. Practice

2. Writing exercise

3.

4.

5.

6.

Page 11. Practice

1. Writing exercise

2.

3.

Page 13. Practice

1. Writing exercise

2.

3.

4.

Page 14. Exercises, Lessons 4–6

1.

2.

3.

Page 15. Ear Training

1.

a.

b.

c.

d.

2.

3.

Page 17. Practice

1.

Page 18. Practice

1.

Page 19

2.

Page 20. Practice

1.

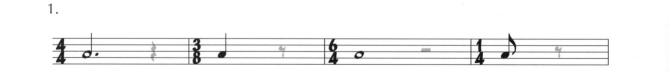

2.

Page 21. Exercises, Lessons 7–9, Ear Training

1.

a.

b.

2.

a.

b.

3.

a.

b.

Page 22

1.

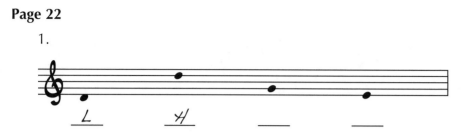

Page 24. Practice

1. Writing exercise

2.

3.

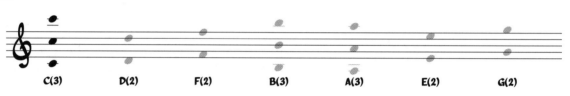

4.

Page 25. Practice

1. Writing exercise

Page 26. Practice

2.

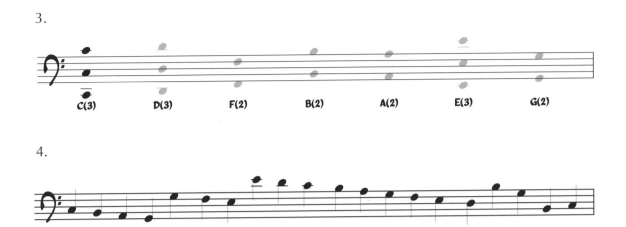

3.

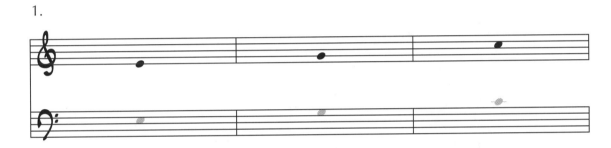

4.

Page 28. Practice

1.

2.

3.

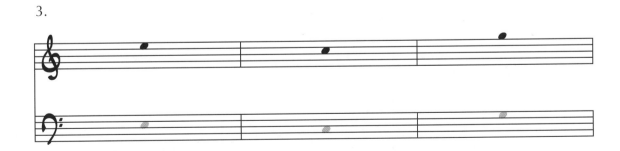

4.

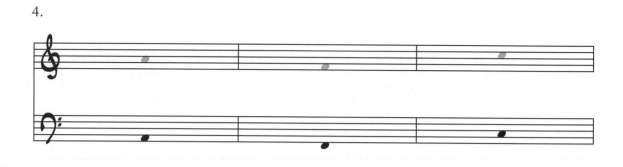

Page 31. Practice

1.

2.

Page 32. Practice

1. Writing exercise

2. Writing exercise

Page 33. Practice

1.

Page 34. Practice

2.

Page 34. Exercises, Lessons 10–16

1.

2.

Page 35

3.

Ear Training

1.

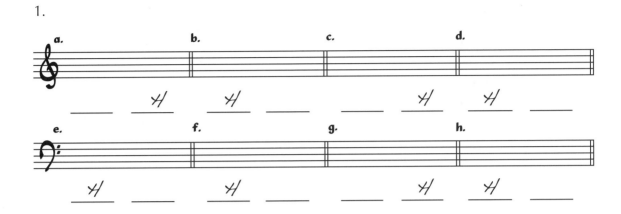

Page 36

2.

Page 38. Practice

1.

2.

3.

4.

Page 40. Practice

1.

2.

Page 42. Practice

1.

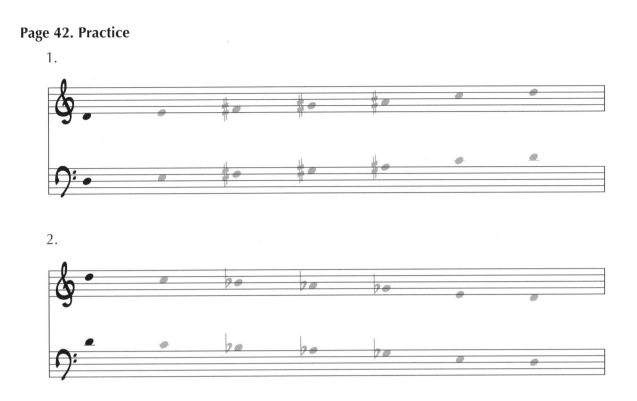

2.

Page 43. Exercises, Lessons 17–19

1.

Ear Training

1. (a) whole (b) half (c) half (d) whole (e) half (f) whole (g) whole (h) half
2. (a) whole tone (b) chromatic (c) whole tone (d) whole tone

Page 45. Practice

1.

2.

Page 47. Practice

1.

2.

Page 48. Practice

1.

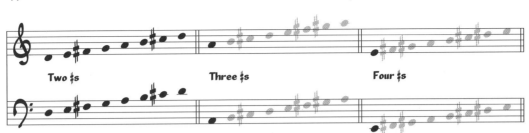

2.

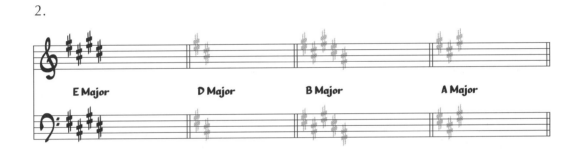

Page 49

1.

2.

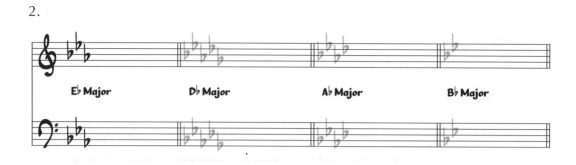

Page 50: Exercises, Lessons 20–25

Page 51. Ear Training

1.

2.

Page 53. Practice

1.

Major

Natural Minor

Major

Natural Minor

Page 55. Practice

2.

Major — Relative Minor

Major — Relative Minor

Major — Relative Minor

Major — Relative Minor

Major — Relative Minor

Page 56. Practice

1.

Page 57: Exercises, Lessons 24–26

1.

5-Sol   *3-Me*   *6-Le*

Ear Training

1. (a) major (b) minor (c) minor (d) major

2. (a) minor (b) major (c) minor (d) major

Page 59. Practice

1.

F Minor: Natural   Harmonic

G Minor: Natural   Harmonic

D Minor: Natural   Harmonic

B Minor: Natural   **Harmonic**

A Minor: Natural   **Harmonic**

E Minor: Natural   **Harmonic**

Page 61. Practice

1.

G Minor: Natural   **Melodic**

B Minor: Natural   **Melodic**

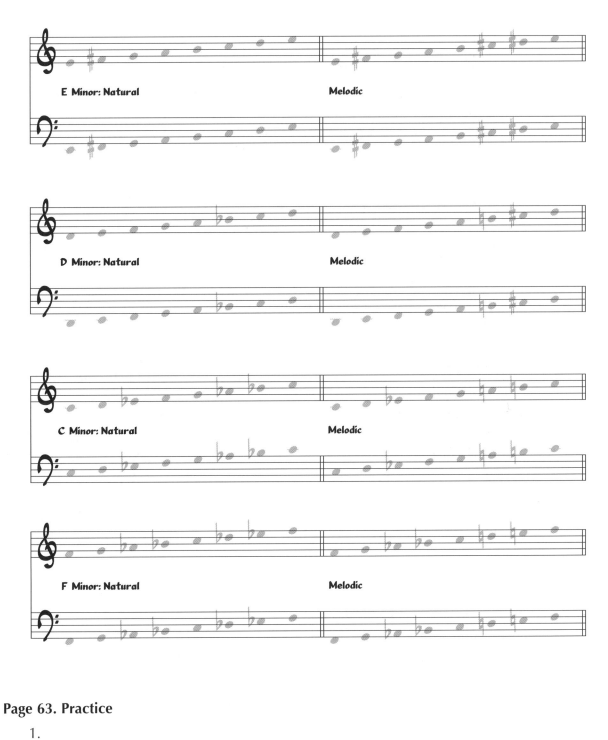

Page 63. Practice

1.

D Minor: Ascending   **Traditional Descending**   **Real Descending**

E Minor: Ascending   **Traditional Descending**   **Real Descending**

Page 64. Practice

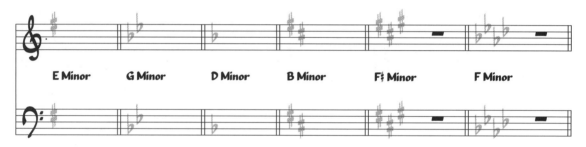

E Minor   **G Minor**   **D Minor**   **B Minor**   **F♯ Minor**   **F Minor**

Page 65. Exercises, Lessons 27–30

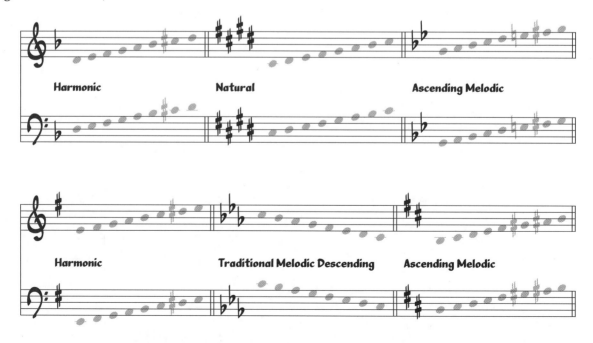

Harmonic   **Natural**   **Ascending Melodic**

Harmonic   **Traditional Melodic Descending**   **Ascending Melodic**

Real Melodic Descending   **Natural**   **Real Melodic Descending**

Page 66. Ear Training

1. (a) natural (b) harmonic (c) harmonic (d) natural

2. (a) real melodic (b) traditional melodic (c) real melodic (d) traditional melodic

3. (a) harmonic (b) natural (c) traditional melodic (d) harmonic (e) natural
   (f) traditional melodic (g) harmonic (h) real melodic

Page 68. Practice

1.

2.

3.

Page 69. Practice

1.

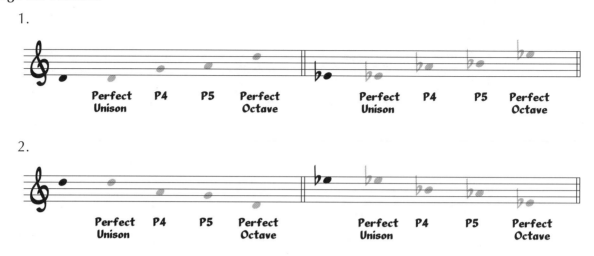

2.

Page 70. Practice

3.

4.

Page 71. Practice

1.

2.

3.

Page 72. Practice

1.

2.

3.

Page 73. Practice

1.

2.

3.

Page 74. Practice

1.

2.

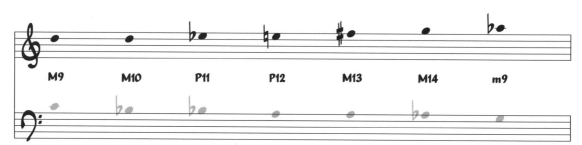

3.

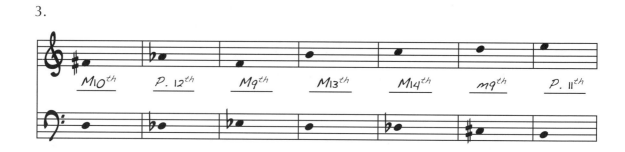

Page 75. Exercises, Lessons 31-36

1.

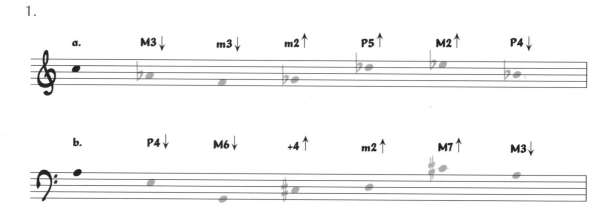

2.

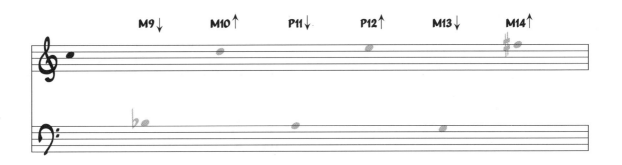

Ear Training

1. (a) P5 (b) m3 (c) M6 (d) P4 (e) m2 (f) M7

2. (a) minor (b) major (c) minor (d) major

Page 76

3. (a) major (b) minor (c) major (d) minor

4. (a) perfect (b) augmented (c) perfect (d) augmented

5. (a) perfect (b) diminished (c) diminished (d) perfect

6. (a) minor (b) major (c) major (d) minor

7. (a) major (b) minor (c) major (d) minor

About the Author

Paul Schmeling, Chair Emeritus of the Piano Department at Berklee College of Music, is a master pianist, interpreter, improviser, and arranger. He has inspired countless students since he began teaching at Berklee in 1961. He has performed or recorded with jazz greats such as Clark Terry, Rebecca Parris, George Coleman, Carol Sloane, Frank Foster, Art Farmer, Herb Pomeroy, Phil Wilson, Dick Johnson, and Slide Hampton. In the 1990s, the Paul Schmeling Trio released two inventive and critically acclaimed albums, interpreting the music of Hoagy Carmichael and songs associated with Frank Sinatra. He is the co-author of the *Berklee Practice Method: Keyboard* (Berklee Press 2001) and *Instant Keyboard* (Berklee Press 2002). He also is the author and instructor of four online courses on Berkleemusic.com, *Music Theory 101, 201, and 301,* and *Berklee Keyboard Method.* Visit the www.berkleemusic.com Web site to learn more.